So You Want to Be a
REAL ESTATE AGENT

a look before you leap handbook

by

Bill Drenik

authorHOUSE

1663 LIBERTY DRIVE, SUITE 200
BLOOMINGTON, INDIANA 47403
(800) 839-8640
www.authorhouse.com

First published by AuthorHouse 11/08/04

ISBN: 1-4184-7323-5 (sc)

Library of Congress Control Number: 2004094589

Printed in the United States of America
Bloomington, Indiana

This book is printed on acid-free paper.

Introduction

Luxury cars, designer clothes, first class restaurants, travel, vacations, expensive homes, country clubs and of course, high income will be yours when you become a Real Estate Agent.

No more punching the time clock or working the swing shift. From now on, you're the boss. You'll spend your days listing and selling homes and the evenings and weekends entertaining.

In just a few weeks or months, you will become a highly trained and generously compensated, card carrying member of the socially elite. You'll be rubbing elbows on a daily basis with Doctors, Lawyers, Corporate Presidents, Directors and executives. Bankers and financial advisors will meet with you on a regular basis. Before too long, you'll begin to consider time shares, vacation homes and early retirement.

<u>Congratulations</u> on your decision to become a real estate agent.

From this point on, this handbook will give you a <u>realistic</u> perspective of what a real estate agents life is like, what you can truly expect, and what you must do to succeed.

High expectations may be shattered but determination will prevail. If after reading this handbook you decide real estate may not be right for you, you will have lost nothing but if you are still with me at the end, you will have absorbed the untold secret to success. You will be prepared, determined and unstoppable.

Real estate is not for everyone. Find out if it's right for you.

Table of Contents

First things first

Before you can begin practicing real estate, you must first obtain a real estate license within the state you are practicing. The division of real estate in each individual state has established the required classes you must successfully complete prior to sitting for your license examination. Generally, these classes consist of Real estate principals and practices, Real estate law, Appraisal and Finance. These courses are normally offered at the college level and may also be available through a local real estate training center.

Please note; the classes are intended to give you a <u>general knowledge</u> of real estate and to awaken you to the complexities of the business. Most classes can be taken in a very short period of time and can usually be taken simultaneously. You will have to be alert, pay attention, take notes and study. Take these classes seriously, they are the foundation of your new career.

Upon completion of all required classes, you will need a sponsoring broker who will hold your license and whom you will represent upon being licensed. Your broker will supply you with an application to take the state exam. You will also need a current picture of yourself, a copy of your transcripts and an application fee. Your broker will submit your application and you will be assigned a date and location to take your state exam. **Be forewarned,** the exam is lengthy and tricky. It will usually consist of multiple choice and math questions. Many training centers offer a refresher crash course just before the exam. You would be wise to take advantage of this.

Note: It is not unusual to fail a portion of the test. If this happens, you must reapply and retake the portion of the test you failed. Don't be discouraged, many of the top agents in real estate today also started with a temporary setback.

Be ***determined*** to succeed. Follow your dreams. A career in real estate can be very rewarding. For sure, it will be challenging. Once licensed, you will have unlimited earning potential. How far you go and how fast you get there will be totally up to you.

Study hard, be determined, get your license and go for it! You are about to enter the world of real estate.

<u>Now that you're licensed</u>

Congratulations! You did it! Your hard work, diligence, sacrifice and commitment has finally paid off. **You are now a Real Estate Agent.** Whether you passed you're state exam on the first try, or it took several attempts, you have accomplished your goal. You have been force fed real estate facts and figures, been scared half out of your wits about agency, lead base paint, state disclosures and liability. You've struggled through an appraisal and can hopefully remember the number of square feet in an acre. You are ready and raring to go!

Through you're enthusiasm and willingness to share the fact that you were taking 'real estate classes' with every friend, relative, enemy and stranger you've ran across, you've probably assembled a list of people who would buy a particular type of property from you, if you could find it at the right price.

You can't wait to get started. You can hardly contain yourself, you're so looking forward to your first day.

Lay out you're clothes, shine your shoes, pack your briefcase with calculator, tape measure, clip board, pens, paper, calendar, pictures of the wife / husband and kids and of course, your list of buyers. Get a good nights rest, tomorrow promises to be an exciting beginning and you are ready!

First day

Board of Realtors? MLS? Computers, faxes, Company policy? Co-brokes, listing files, floor time, title companies?

What's going on here? Internet, websites, meetings, training, documentation and more documentation. Cell phones, voice mail, virtual tours, phone systems, pagers. Code of ethics, legal defense? Promissory notes and who's on first? Exclusive representation, Buyers agent? Sellers agent? dual agent? Signs, riders, marketing tools. Farming systems, Order a legal? postcard system, input forms & CMA's? Make the appointment, record the call, call the agent, "Don't cut the commission", yadda, yadda, yadda.

All right, enough of that. Let's get serious.
You will quickly come to the realization that although you are licensed to sell real estate, you have no idea how to go about it. Funny isn't it? First you get the license and then you learn the trade. Aren't you glad Doctors don't do it this way? Anyway, ***resolve yourself to the fact that you now have a license to learn.*** You will continue to learn for as long as you are in the business for it is constantly changing.

Have patience. Take little steps. You will find that, much to your surprise, Real Estate is extremely complicated. You will at times feel as if you're going nowhere fast. That's normal, trust me.

You will be learning each and every day. Each day you'll become more prepared. Before too long you'll begin to feel confident and you will actually begin to formulate a strategy. ***Success will come, but not before failure.***

Don't give up! Be determined and be careful.

Remember that you are your own boss. You must discipline yourself to learn. You must motivate yourself to work. No one will be telling you what to do forever.

You will quickly take note that your broker, manager, trainer and successful peers will encourage you to try particular techniques that have proven to be successful.
Others will discourage you from doing those same techniques. Their reasoning varying from, "I've been in this business for umpteen years and I never have done that", to "I tried that once and it didn't work." or "I don't have time for that" etc. etc.

Be careful whom you learn from, ***It's crowded at the bottom!***

It has been statistically proven that 10% of the agents do 90% of the business. Let me repeat that, **10% of the real estate agents in the business do 90% of the business in real estate.**
What about the rest of the agents? Each and every one had the very same aspirations of success in the beginning, the very same dreams and expectations. What happened? Simply put, they were discouraged by their peers. After all, misery loves company.

To succeed, you must decide that you ***will be successful.*** Remember you are your own boss now.

Your time is your money. The more time you spend focused on the business of real estate, the more money you will make. Period!

Real estate agents come in all sizes, shapes, colors, ages and personalities with backgrounds from all different walks of life. They are however, a very special breed, at least the ones who survive the first year. They thrive on pressure and are motivated by stress and frustration. They expect, and accept rejection and in fact, look forward to it in certain situations. They accept failure and learn from it. They usually receive more gratification from a job well done than from the payment they receive. They wear many hats. They must be many things to many people and they manage brilliantly. They love what they're doing and can't get enough.

You've probably heard someone say that it usually takes about 6 months before you begin to make money in real estate. With some exceptions, that's a pretty accurate statement.

In the following pages, I will share some vital information with you that will not only get you earning commissions sooner, but will guarantee your future success. It won't be easy, but you can do it!

Let's get started.

Where to find business

It is important to begin to tell everyone you know, and everyone you meet or do business with from now on, that you are a licensed real estate agent.

Opportunities are everywhere and people love to send business your way, however, they must know you're in the business or you will miss many opportunities.

Of course your immediate family will know, as will your close friends. That is an excellent start but don't forget your extended family, Aunts, Uncles, Cousins, in-laws, neighbors, waitresses, grocers, bankers, cab drivers, cashiers, car salesmen, builders, your children's teachers, Doctors, Lawyers, CPA's, etc. everyone is a potential buyer or seller, and everyone that you know knows someone that you don't know.

This is the beginning of your sphere of influence. If you keep your name and occupation fresh in the minds of these people, they will remember you and refer you every time someone mentions the possibility of buying or selling real estate.

Let me interject right now that you are not limited to any particular area, you are licensed within your state and that is your boundary. In addition, your company will have a referral program that will allow you to refer a customer to another real estate company in any state or any area of your own state, and in most cases, anywhere in the world. Think about that!

Maybe your relatives in Florida have a friend that will be relocating to California. You can refer their friend to a Florida Realtor and to a California Realtor and get paid when the customer sells their home and again when they buy another. The possibilities are endless. Retirees move south constantly. Someone you know knows someone making those plans right now.

Keep your ears open for referral opportunities. All you need is a name, telephone number and destination. That's easy money.

Read the newspaper. You will find endless leads there.
People are constantly on the move. Company expansions mean new people will be hired. These new people will need housing. Layoffs may mean people will be moving. People get married, they need housing, People get divorced, usually a house gets sold. Families get bigger and up-size their home, the kids grow up and leave and families downsize again. People inherit homes and land and many times sell it. These estates are profit centers. People get transferred and have to sell or buy. Other people may find themselves in a financial bind for one reason or another and will have to sell.
Business is everywhere, but you must recognize the opportunity.

Another source of business in the newspaper is of course the Homes for Sale section of the classified ads.
This is a tremendous source of business. These are Fsbo's. (For sale by owners) A high percentage of these will eventually list their home with a real estate agent. In addition, many

will agree to pay a commission if you provide a customer who buys their home.

The important thing to remember is that you must know the inventory of available homes for sale, whether listed or unlisted.

Absolutely everyone is a potential client or customer. You will miss many opportunities unless you are constantly and continuously letting people know that you are a licensed agent. In a very large way, that is your job now. Come to grips with that.

You are no longer an employee. You are now an independent contractor. *You must generate your own business.*

You must give the impression and create the perception that you are the agent to call for any and all real estate needs. More on that later.

By now, you're beginning to realize there's more to this than meets the eye. Well, were just at the tip of the iceberg. As I've stated, Real Estate is a very complex business. However, it's simply a matter of giving yourself the time to learn.

You can realize your dreams. You <u>can</u> become a top agent and you <u>can</u> do it in a very reasonable amount of time. But you must take charge!

Keep forefront in your mind that only 10% of all of the agents in the business of Real Estate do 90% of the business. You must make a choice. Which group will you fall into?

Let's get specific now. Where should you focus? How do you get started?

___Polish up___

Appearance is important. Remember that you are a professional. To create an image of professionalism, keep yourself well groomed, clean, and neatly dressed. Don't go overboard with jewelry, makeup and fancy clothes. Realtor pins and pin on jewelry are appropriate for women and work silently on your behalf. Go easy on perfumes and colognes, you don't want to be offensive.

Your image establishes your credibility. Dress appropriately. First impressions are lasting.

Keep your car clean, at least the exterior. (The inside of a real estate agents car usually looks like the aftermath of a nuclear blast)

Learn to listen. Ask your customers and clients appropriate questions regarding their needs and listen to their response. You will quickly learn to, read between the lines, and will be able to help them more effectively.

Be prepared. Know the market. Facts, figures and information are your tools now. You must keep them sharp! Never go on an appointment without first doing the research.

The entire above can be accomplished very easily. *You are creating a perception of professionalism. By doing so, you are already giving yourself an advantage over some of your peers.*

Bill Drenik

I don't mean to be harsh, but this handbook is intended to give an advantage. You are never really selling real estate. You are always selling yourself, and your service. 99% of the time, you do not own the home you will be selling nor will you be interested in buying it

You have no product! You will either be hired by a client to represent your brokerage in marketing their home, (Listing) or represent a customer in their home search. (Purchase) Your function is to represent either, and sometimes both. You will facilitate the intricate details, arrange marketing, showings, inspections, appraisals, financing, etc., whatever the case may be.

You will act, as counselor to your client but you will never make a decision regarding the sale of their home. You will prepare documentation for your buyers and sellers and will be responsible for knowing, and explaining thoroughly, the context of the documents you are asking them to sign.

Note: I cannot express enough, the importance of knowing the context of the documents. Many agents start out in the business simply having the client or customer, fill in the blanks. They will quickly become enveloped in turmoil, and may soon become element to a lawsuit. **Ignorance is no excuse.** Before you ever have a customer or client sign any documentation whatsoever, You must be able to explain the ramifications of their acceptance. These are binding contracts, enforceable by law.

On a positive note, knowing and being able to explain the documentation will once again give you a distinct advantage over many of your peers. Reviewing and understanding each and every document will give you tremendous insights into the profession.

<u>You must do it!</u> No one can do it for you. You can't put them under your pillow and absorb information through osmosis. These things take time at first, but this is time well spent. I know you're anxious to get started, you will not be losing money, but increasing your earning potential dramatically.

By now you're probably sweating bullets wondering if this is right for you. Keep reading the best is yet to come.

Survival rate

Assuming you took your state exam at the same time as 500 others in your state. About 60% or 300 probably passed. Some will test again until they pass others will quit.

Let's take the 300 that passed. They will be distributed throughout the state in such a manner that their presence will hardly be noticed.

Out of the 300, approx. 50% or 150 will still be in the business after 1 year. Within 5 years, approximately 50% of these survivors will remain is the business, or 75 remaining agents.

Whether you survive or not will be totally up to your commitment to learn the business from the ground up. I can assure you that there will always be room for quality professionals in the business, and that their income level will always be exceptional, unlimited, and constant.

Rest assured that the number of agents getting into the business will be dwindling, but the quality of these individuals will be improving. People will always need housing, that's a given. ***The demand for quality professionals is constantly increasing.*** Opportunities are endless and will always be there.

You must be willing to accept and embrace change. You must be able to keep pace with an ever changing world and the tremendous advances and improvements in technology. Typically, your company will have implemented various marketing programs that are designed to enhance your ability to obtain listings and to guarantee that your time spent with potential buyers is productive. **These programs must be utilized.** They will give you an advantage in the marketplace and will give you a professional distinction, save you time, make you money and generate continuous business. Take the time to review the different marketing tools available. Ask your broker or manager to help you decide which of these programs will best benefit you. As you progress, there will always be an abundance of tools available which you may be interested in purchasing. These might include lap top computers, special top producer software, marketing newsletters, telemarketing programs and many others. You will also want to utilize your companies Internet site(s), where you will find a vast array of beneficial information for both yourself and your clients.

As you can see, to survive in the world of real estate, you must commit to continuously learn, improve and change. A reasonable amount of adjustment time is expected, but you will soon become a knowledgeable professional. If you're still with me, you just might have what it takes.

Now let's begin to look into the two phases of the business that put the bread on the table, **<u>Listing</u> and <u>Selling.</u>**

Listings

There is no quicker way to the top of your chosen profession than through your efforts as a Listing agent.

Lister's are leaders, they control the inventory and therefore control the market. I will guarantee you that the top agents in your area, no matter where that may be, are the agents that have mastered the techniques necessary to secure listings.

Think about this, when you successfully secure a listing, and submit it into the local multiple listing service, (mls) you are immediately exposing it to every agent belonging to that mls. Many of them have accumulated a list of buyers looking for a certain type, style, size, or priced home in a particular area or areas. If your listing matches the Buyers parameters, the agent will call them immediately and set up an appointment for them to view the home.

Remember, every agent has buyers, Including you, If the home you list meets the specifications of your buyer, they will obviously have first choice. If they like it, and write an acceptable offer, you will have made a commission on both the listing and the sale. That's the way to make **big money fast!**

Another advantage to being the listing agent is that the inquiries on that listing are usually directed to you. After all, your name and number are on the sign rider in front of the house. Your name and telephone number will usually be included in any advertising.

19

The seller is instructed to refer any inquiries about the home to you. You are the listing agent, you know the most about the home. If at all possible, the customer will make every effort to speak with you. ***If you are going to be a top agent, you must focus on listings.*** Consider listings to be the fuel that runs your real estate machine. Here's a typical scenario:

An agent lists 5 homes per month. Out of these five 2 are sold by another agent, and 2 are sold by the Listing agent. Of the 2 the Listing agent sells, one may have to sell their home in order to buy. Guess whose going to list their home?

On a continuing basis, This agents focus is entirely on listing homes. Of course he'll do his share of selling but his focus remains on listing. By listing 5 homes in the example above, the Listing agent will receive commission checks for 4 listings and for 2 sales and will have acquired a bonus listing that is all but guaranteed to sell, and sell quickly. Multiply this typical month times 12 and you can easily see why the Listing agent is a top agent.

Let me assure you that the above example is very realistic, and well within your reach. Many top agents average much higher numbers.

You see, listings are the fuel that keep the machine running smoothly. Without fuel, it will begin to sputter, spit, and eventually quit. Let's look further into being an effective listing agent.

<u>*Listing tips and techniques*</u>

In the previous example, the Listing agent averaged 5 listings per month. Let's break that down to 1.25 listings per week. Now let's face it, you can do 1.25 things per week, can't you? That's 1 listing every 4 days if you're working a 5-day week. Assuming you work 8 hours per day, that's 32 hours per listing. Once you've acquired a listing it will take approx. 8 hours to process it from filling out the listing agreements to the time your ready to submit it to the MLS. That leaves 24 working hours to get a listing. (3 days) OK. now you're ready, where do you start?

Listings are found in many places, but let's focus on 2 in particular. We'll discuss other areas as we go along.

1. Expired Listings - Why do you want an expired listing? Because you're a top agent! *Because you know that owner wants to sell his house, and you know he is willing to pay a commission.*

In all likelihood, the seller will have a sour taste in his mouth for real estate agents in general since he's just been through 6 months without communication with an agent that "hardly ever showed the house."
This, is music to your ears. As a top agent, you must learn to listen, this seller will quickly tell you what he didn't like about his last experience, and exactly what you will need to do to please him. <u>You're halfway there!</u>

21

You will find that if you listen with compassion and understanding of his displeasure, he will begin to warm up to you. Don't push for the listing, the last thing this guy needs is for you to begin making promises or giving him false hope. He's already fallen for that once and I can assure you he will cut you off at the first hint of a repeat performance.

<u>Talk with him.</u> You'll find things in common. Before you know it, He'll be asking you why his house didn't sell. Now you have an opportunity to make a preliminary appointment to view the house. After all, you're a professional. You couldn't possibly know the problem without seeing it, could you?

Make this appointment non-committal, no obligation for him to list with you, or you to take the listing. However, ask questions about the house. Age, condition, location, bedrooms, baths, amenities, how long has he lived there? Is there a mortgage? Are there any problems with the house? Where will he be moving too? When would he like to be there? Why is he selling?

Don't worry, he'll be glad to share this information with you. He understands you'll need it.

Now that you've got the information you need, and have made an appointment to meet the seller, you must *research, research, research.* You want to go prepared to get the listing.

Without knowing the house, location or seller, you all- ready know the reason the house did not sell. Don't you? Well maybe not, at least not yet. Without a doubt, and **without exception**, <u>the reason that sellers house hasn't sold is the</u>

<u>asking price.</u> **Burn that in your brain.** That will be true <u>100%</u> of the time.

To sell a house or anything for that matter, the price must be competitive when compared to a similar house or product. No exceptions!

You're job now is to research comparable properties that have recently sold and competing listings on the market today. You must be able to share this information in a *professional manner* and in a *convincing way*. **<u>Without waffling!</u>**

Remember you're trying to help. There is absolutely no chance that you will help this seller if you aren't able to agree on a competitive price to list his home. In fact, taking this listing overpriced will only drive the eventual selling price even lower. It is far better to be able to share the information, facts and figures with this seller and leave without the listing than to take a listing that is grossly overpriced.

By establishing your professionalism in this way, the seller will understand that you mean business. It may take a day or two for the seller to accept the facts, and there is a chance he will again list it 'overpriced' with someone else, but if he does, you will have lost nothing.

Remember you're a top agent and a listing leader. You list homes to sell, not just to have a listing. You can bet, the agent who previously had the above listing was a member of the 90% club, you know, the 90% that do 10% of the business. Check the MLS and call on expired listings daily. You'll get your share of the expired listings, and you'll sell them! This is a continuous source of business.

Bill Drenik

Each and every day, listings expire. It would seem likely that every agent would be calling on them, wouldn't it? Don't bet on it. A very small percentage of agents actually call on expired listing owners. I'd confidently say, less than 5%.

Real Estate is a percentage game. No matter what you do, or how you do it, you will always get more negative responses than positive. **<u>Get over it!</u>** That's part of the business.

<u>Don't take it personally.</u> In fact, learn to look forward to rejection. After all, each time you're rejected, you're that much closer to being accepted.

If you are successful 10 times out of 100 calls to expired listing owners, you will have been rejected 90 times. However, you will have arranged 10 appointments and probably acquired 8 or more listings. **<u>There's a lot of commission dollars in 8 listings.</u>**
You did very little to acquire them other than checking the mls, looking up telephone numbers and making a 'warm' call. Don't you think it's worth it?

By the way, some of the owners that had originally rejected your attempt to discuss their expired listing will be calling you back. They will decide to re-list, and obviously want to list with a professional.

There is another source of business staring you in the face each and every day. The approach is slightly different, but the percentage of success is even higher. Let's check it out!

2. The For Sale By Owner - (Fsbo) Once again, we're dealing with a group of Homeowners that have made it perfectly clear that, <u>they intend to sell</u>.

For a professional, this is real estate heaven. A very high percentage of these owners will eventually list their Home with a real estate agent.

No one can blame a homeowner for trying to sell on his or her own. The small percentage that does succeed should be applauded. The majority however will normally find the experience frustrating, time consuming, stressful, exhausting and futile. They usually exhaust their efforts in a short time and then decide to 'call the real estate company.' With a little effort, you can be sure that when the time does come to call an agent, you're the lucky winner!

Before we look into what you must do to 'get the call', let's look at the telltale signs of the eventual listings.

Signage - The type, size and location of the owner's sign says an awful lot about the owner. If the owner has hired a professional sign painter, or has a 4x8 illuminated sign in his front yard, that usually means he's digging in, expecting you, and has enough verbal opposition ammunition to hold you off for quite some time. This guys tough! He's going to sell this home by himself come hell or high water!

Actually the chances of this owner selling himself are going to be quite slim. He's probably overpriced and knows it. He will probably be his own worst enemy if and when anyone does make him an offer, and to be sure, will never admit you might be able to help.

Believe it or not, this is a possible listing opportunity. It probably won't happen for several years, probably about the time he runs out of touch up paint for his sign, but there is a possibility that he'll warm up to you by then. On the bright side, the market will have almost caught up with his price. You might have a chance.

How about the drugstore 'For Sale' sign hammered into the front yard? Now this sounds promising. **This owner needs you.** He has boldly placed a sign in his front yard and is probably in there looking out the window at you right now. Of course, in order to read his sign, you've got to pull off the road, get out of your car, walk up to his sign, and decipher his hieroglyphics. This is probably a busy street, and the only people willing to risk life and limb to get the telephone number are top real estate professionals like you.

You definitely can help this owner. It will take some time, but not a great deal. What's important is that you make the call, introduce yourself, <u>go meet him personally</u>, and <u>keep in touch weekly.</u>

Many times, an owner will place a sign in their yard that simply says 'For Sale', this sign will probably be nailed to a tree, or directly to the house, or the sign may be in the window.

There will probably not even be a telephone number. ***<u>Run!, don't walk, to this front door.</u>*** **This owner is ready now!** He knows he needs help, he just doesn't know who to call. He has probably lived in the house for years, and has no idea what it might be worth.

Your confidence and professionalism will quickly be appreciated and rewarded with another listing.

Another sign to look for is the one with an out of the area telephone number. This will probably mean the home is vacant. Perhaps the owner has been transferred, it may be an estate, there may be a pending divorce etc. One thing is for certain. This home will be sold! The person out of town will not be willing to drive to town to show the house, at least not for long. They will be concerned about security, vandalism & theft. They will have ongoing costs they'd rather not have. Utilities, heat, insurance etc. They want it sold, and they want it sold *now*!

You'll want to offer your help in a reassuring and professional way. They will need to trust you. Compassion is required patience is rewarded. *Another listing for your inventory!*

These are just a few 'tips' regarding signs. You'll learn many more in your career.

OK, now let's read between the lines on a few real estate ads.

Look for telltale signs of desperation. 'No Realtors' usually means this seller has had a previous bad experience. He probably had his property listed with a weak agent, undoubtedly a bottom percentile agent, or with a friend or relative. In all likelihood, they took the listing knowing full well the chances of it selling were very slim.

Either the owner ignored their advice regarding the price, or, was never given any. His overpriced listing sat stagnating while properties around it were selling like hot cakes. He had little or no showings, no one came to the open house, his agent never called him, and of course he wasn't satisfied with the advertising.

27

You've got your work cut out for you here. A phone call will never do. He'll probably slam the phone down on your ear. However, I would advise a personal visit. Remember you have nothing at all to lose and everything to gain. Your mission, should you decide to accept it, is to personally introduce yourself. Feel free to wave a white flag. Let him know you read his ad, aren't there to solicit the listing, but would like to be able to tell your customers about it, 'no obligation'. He won't trust you, at least, at first. In fact, he may slam the door in your face. Knock again, give your card and thank him.

Tell him you'll be in touch, and leave. Give this man room, you've got plenty of time. Call him in a week and remind him who you are. Ask if He's willing to show you the house yet. If not, that's OK. Call again the next week. Keep calling him every week. He'll recognize your persistence. Soon, you'll be on a first name basis. Eventually, you'll be invited over to 'have a look'.

Carefully evaluate the property, then decide if you can help. **Be Careful.** Do not take this listing unless it's priced right.

'Realtors Welcome' - Don't let this phrase fool you. They're not intending to list, they do however want to sell. This is a definite 'must see'.

Although the owners are allowing this home to be shown through an agent, most agents will simply ignore this home. Don't make that mistake. Make an appointment, introduce yourself and view the home. There is an excellent chance a customer you're working with now, or in the near future might be interested in it.

You're brokerage will have an 'unlisted property' form that you should have the owner sign when you preview the home. It simply states you will be representing a buyer in the sale of the home and that the seller will agree to pay a commission of _____%

Go for a full 7%. There's room to negotiate, of course, but if you can get 7%, it's the same as selling your own listing.

Be careful, There is a good possibility that this seller will list soon. You'll want to get the listing but it's always hard to get a full commission once you've agreed to take less. Remember, once it's listed, it's open to Co-broke sales.

Usually, an owner will run an ad in a local paper for a week or so. They'll field many calls, probably show the house a few times, maybe hold it open on Sunday etc. Their anticipation of a quick sale will soon pass. They'll begin to resent the calls, get defensive about their Home and tired of being tied to it. Before long, they'll consider giving it to an agent. **You'll want to be their agent!**
Call them with encouragement. Help them all you can, at arms length. Be professional! You're not trying to make friends now <u>this is your livelihood.</u>

Remember you're trying to sell <u>yourself.</u> A weekly call of encouragement a reminder of forms and disclosures required by your State Division Of Real Estate, a lead base paint pamphlet etc. These are all positive gestures that will silently build a trust. This owner will be comforted by your concern, impressed with your tenacity, and influenced by your professionalism. You'll get the call when they're ready to list. You can count on that.

Things to remember - When an owner hires you to 'list' their home, understand what that means. They are hiring your company to *market the home.*

You're responsibility as the listing agent is to seek and acquire the listing, properly prepare all documentation, gather the necessary information to complete the MLS input form(s), write alluring and descriptive ads, ensure proper signs are posted and communicate with the sellers on a regular basis.

You are representing them! You are their counselor, co-ordinator and communicator. They are counting on you, and you alone to keep them informed of showings, comments, interest, offers and negotiations.

Nothing, and I mean nothing, will upset an owner more than lack of communication from their agent.

Find out how and how often, the seller wants you to communicate. In person? By telephone? Voice mail? In writing? e-mail?

Let them know if you're receiving calls on their property. Call every agent that shows the Home and get customer feedback. Relay the information, all of it, good or bad, to the seller. Make suggestions that might make the home more attractive to a buyer.

If feedback indicates the Home is too cluttered, busy, gaudy, dirty, small, large, or expensive, you have an obligation to tell the seller.

Don't make excuses for the buyer. The seller needs every bit of information you can provide to make necessary adjustments in price or terms in order to generate an acceptable offer.

Your Brokerage will provide an advertising program to expose the property. In addition to the multiple listing services available, your company will make every effort and attempt to expose the property to potential buyers. This will normally consist of newspaper and Internet presentations at a minimum.

Top Agents advertise their own listings. This is a very effective way to market themselves. A personal marketing program is guaranteed to keep your name in people's minds, generate more listings and provide a continuous pool of buyers. **Warning!** A personal marketing plan will immediately increase the demand for your services. *Be prepared to deliver.*

OK, clear your mind. Get a cup of coffee and take a break. We're about to go in an entirely different direction.

Selling

Hopefully, by now you have resolved yourself to become a Top <u>Listing</u> agent. You will find that to be the quickest road from rags to riches.

As a successful listing agent, you will always have an unlimited supply of potential Buyers. You will need to learn the most efficient procedure to sell them the ideal Home. Before we begin, let's look in on a typical 'average' agent and what, in many offices, might be considered normal.

9:15am Monday morning. Ima Agent of Ready Realtors arrives at the office. She is scheduled for 'floor' time from 9:00 AM to 1:00PM. She arranges herself at the floor desk, pours a cup of coffee and heads for the powder room to finish her hair and makeup. She'll grab another cup of coffee, check her mailbox, read the mail, exchange pleasantries and head for her 'post'.

A short time later she receives an 'ad' call. She has the caller on speakerphone because she's just put the first coat on her nails and they're not quite dry yet. She gives the caller the address of the property and asks him to call back if he's interested.

A few minutes later, another call. She puts her girl friend on hold while giving out another address. Meanwhile another call from a co-broke agent who would like to show one of Ready Realtors listings. She puts the agent on hold while finishing up with her girl friend. She says she'll call her back and takes the co-broke agents call. The co-broke agent wants to show Tommy Toplisters Oak St. listing at 5:00 PM

Bill Drenik

on Wednesday. Ima leaves that information on Tommy's voice mail and grabs another cup of coffee.

Now it's time to read the newspaper. After all, she wouldn't want to miss a sale. Another phone call interrupts her while she's balancing her checkbook. She's beginning to get quite aggravated but answers the phone. "Ready Realtors, Ima Agent speaking". She says.

"Yes, this is Bobby Buyer, I called earlier about the Home on Dreamers Drive. I think I'd like to have a look." Just my luck, thinks Ima, I'll probably have to miss my favorite soap opera "When would you like to see it" she groans. "I'm off this afternoon " says Bobby. "How about 3 o'clock"? "That will be fine " smiles Ima, as she realizes Dreamers Drive is just 5 minutes from Glamour Gallery Dept. store. "I'll meet you there at 3."

It's almost 12:00 so Ima decides to leave early. She'll want to 'do lunch' before heading for the Dept. store.

3:10 P.M. - Ima arrives at the Home on Dreamers Drive. She frantically rushes to the door and rings the bell.
Inside she hears Mrs. Seller pointing out every obvious feature of the Home. ...."This is the living room and that's the fireplace. All the built in's in the kitchen will stay with the house." blah blah blah, etc, etc.
"Sorry I'm Late, traffic don't you know" says Ima. (What she really means is, there was a long line at the check out counter) She introduces herself to Mrs. Seller and Bobby. "Thank you for your help Mrs. Seller, I'll let you get back to whatever you were doing" she says. "OK Bob, where would you like to start?" she asks.

34

"Actually, I got here a little early and Mrs. Seller was nice enough to show me the interior. I would like to walk around the Home. By the way, do you have any information that I may take with me? Ima panics, "There should be some here somewhere, why don't you walk around the Home and I'll catch up." Ima frantically searches for the information the listing agent should have left at the home. (Never count on this) Empty handed, she catches up with Bobby. "I'm sorry, the Listing agent is supposed to leave that information here. I'll be sure to tell him you were disappointed."

"All right", says Bobby, "How much is the owner asking for the property?" "$189,900" smiles Ima. "That seems a little high" says Bobby, "How much are the taxes?"

"I'll have to get back to you with that information" groans Ima. "Would you happen to know the school system?" asks Bobby. "I'm pretty sure it's Future Leaders, but I'll have to check on that also. Do you have any other questions?" moans Ima.

"Tell you what," says Bobby, "I'd like to bring someone else to look at the House. Can you meet us tomorrow at 5:30?" "Absolutely!" shrieks Ima, excited about a second showing. "I'll definitely have more information then."

As she's setting up tomorrow's appointment with Mrs. Seller. Ima can't help but notice Bobby's 1978 Pinto. Mmmm, must be his work car. She thinks.

"I think He's really interested" she tells Mrs. Seller. "He asked an awful lot of questions." An anxious Mrs. Seller smiles.

Bill Drenik

Tuesday, 5:15 P.M.- Ima arrives early, views the Home, verifies the school system with the owners and patiently waits for Bobby. *She is ready*.

She has previewed the disclosures, memorized the input sheet, knows the taxes, assessments, median temperature, average rainfall and of course, distance to the department stores. She meets Bobby and his girlfriend Joan at the front door. Gives them the grand tour, answers every question, points out the particulars and backs off. She knows there is an interest but she doesn't want to push. She gives then time to talk amongst themselves.

"We're interested," says Bobby. "We'd like to make an offer." "Great." smiles Ima, "Let's go back to the office."

Ima drives back extremely slow. Not only does she not want to lose them but she's trying to remember what to do next. Her hands are wringing wet and her makeup begins to run. She silently begins to pray that someone else will be there..................

They arrive at the office.- No ones here, Ima thinks, I'm doomed. "Pull yourself together" she tells herself. "You can do this."

They follow her in and she shows them to the closing room. She turns to them and says, "Please have a seat, I'll be with you in a minute. Would you like a cup of coffee?"

They both look absolutely shocked. Eyes wide open, jaws drop simultaneously, they look at each other and back at Ima, shaking their heads. "No thank you" Bobby says. "Very well then, I'll be right back." Smiles Ima.

They seem a little nervous, she thinks, I hope they don't change their mind. She hears whispering and almost hysterical laughter coming from the closing room. That's better, she thinks, I knew they really liked that House.

A few minutes later Ima returns, confident she has gathered the correct documentation necessary to write the offer.

"All right then, let's get started." she says.

"We'd like to offer $140,000 says Bobby. "We really want the House, but only if we can get it at that price."...............

Needless to say, this saga went on. Ima dejectedly muddled through, the offer was presented to a very disappointed Mr. & Mr. Seller. They agreed to counter the offer at $185,000. It was not accepted.

Weeks later, after showing Bobby and Joan 22 Homes and writing 3 additional unacceptable offers, Ima receives a voice mail from Bobby. "Ima , this is Bobby Buyer. I've got great news! Joan and I stopped at a FSBO on Losers Lane. We just fell in love with it. We made the owner an offer and He's accepted it! I wanted to let you know so that you could cancel the 4 showings you have scheduled for us this afternoon. Thanks for all your time and effort. It was uh,...........interesting working with you. I'll be sure to tell all my friends to call you. Hope you understand, we had no choice, the property was unlisted. Thanks again, we'll be seeing you."

A speechless Ima drops the phone. Her thoughts immediately go to the charges she's made on her credit card in anticipation of the 'big' sale. She is devastated.

6 weeks later Ima receives a call from Bobby.

37

"Ima, this is Bobby Buyer, do you remember me?" "Oh yes." sighs Ima, "So how's the new house? "she asks.

"Well that didn't quite work out" he says, "I couldn't qualify on my own because of the bankruptcy I had last year so Joan agreed to co-sign. On the way to the Title company to sign the final papers we had a huge fight about financing 125% of the purchase price and we broke up.
The sellers are really upset because they had bought another house and have hired an attorney to sue me. I'm not a bit worried about it though because I don't have anything to give them. Anyway, I've got another girlfriend now so I'd like to start looking at Houses again. I'm just waiting for the seller to give me back my $1000.00 earnest money deposit. This has been a terrible experience, I should have stuck with you in the first place."

Ima smiles. "It's always better to work with an agent " she says. "There's a great House over on Continuous Circle. I'll set it up for tomorrow."
"Great! " says Bobby. "I'll see you then. Goodbye."
Ima thinks, mmm...........I better call Glamour Gallery. Maybe I'll put those earrings in layaway.

***And so it goes*.................**Obviously, the above scenario is a bit far fetched, but to be sure, there are agents in the business today that relate very closely to Ima's real estate practice.

Although listing opportunities are by far, more desirable. Selling plays an equal role. After all, Listings mean nothing without Buyers. In fact, an agent who concentrates on acquiring Listings will have many more opportunities to sell.

Selling is time consuming. To be effective, you'll need to condense the procedure as much as possible. You also want to be certain the Buyer is serious, loyal and qualified. If, you do it properly, selling is an equally profitable facet of the business. Here are a few tips to get you on the right track.

First contact - Just as before, it is most important to establish your professionalism. You must project a sincere desire and ability to aid the customer on their Home search. *You must be knowledgeable.* They are talking with you for one reason. They want information. You, on the other hand, will need a certain amount of information from the customer as well.

Always get the callers name, e-mail and telephone number, and always be absolutely certain they have yours. Ask questions as you give information, this allows you to determine the buyers wants and needs. (I.e.) The property you've called about has 3 Br's and 1 bath, is that what you're looking for? - The Home is situated on 1/2 acre. Will that be large enough? Do you have children or pets? - You called on a Colonial Home. Is that the style most desirable to you? - This property is in Lake County, is that where you'd like to relocate?

You get the picture. Give and get as much information as possible.
Always ask the question. Are you working with an agent? If so, be cordial, but suggest they call that agent for further information.

If they're not working with another agent, arrange an appointment to meet them. You will have the opportunity to discuss their needs in further detail, explain the benefits of working exclusively with one agent, and describe and explain the different types of representation available to them. They must also acknowledge that you have explained your company's agency policy with them.

Discuss their ability to purchase at first contact as well. <u>*Are they pre- approved?*</u> Above all, before you begin showing Homes to any customer, you must know the price range they can afford. This can be accomplished in a matter of minutes these days. This service is available 7 days a week. A toll free telephone call and 10-20 minutes will assure the buyer that they have the ability to purchase, the price range they should concentrate on, the current interest rate, and the costs involved in the purchase.

Selling Homes takes time. Rarely will a purchaser buy without looking at many Homes first. You can streamline the time by only showing properties in the Buyers price range. When a Buyer is pre-approved, that means the lender will make a loan to the purchaser subject only to appraisal.

Do not confuse pre-approved with pre-qualification. Pre-qualified means the customer has the income required, but their credit has not been checked, their debts have not been determined, employment has not been verified, and that a multitude of other obstacles may surface forcing the lender to reject the loan.

Have the buyer pre-approved. This service, which you can arrange, will save you tremendous disappointments and more importantly, time. Remember time is money.

A Buyer may think they are able to purchase based upon the fact that they have a decent income, and pay their bills. This is music to a lenders ear, but the lender must consider much more.

Income to debt ratio, credit scoring, time on the job, late payment history, past bankruptcies or foreclosures. Is the buyer paying or receiving alimony or child support? Has He made any major purchases recently? Are there any garnishments or judgments against him? How much of the buyer's income is derived from working overtime? If they are currently renting, how long have they been at their current address? Do they move frequently? How many credit cards does he own? Etc.

These are questions a lender will ask and verify. **Don't waste your time. Have the buyer pre-approved!**

OK. Let's look at a hypothetical situation. You've met a potential customer face to face. You've determined they are looking for a 4 bedroom 2 bath ranch with a family room, a full finished basement an attached 2 car garage. They would like to have a minimum of 5 acres, be within 5 minutes of the interstate and they would prefer a home less than 10 years old. They are pre-approved for a mortgage loan of $150,000 but want to stay under $125,000. This will be there first home. They are currently renting a 2 BR, 1 bath duplex. Their apartment is on the second floor, and the structure is

75 years old. They live in the city, both adults work, and they have a teenage son and daughters, 6 and 4 years old.

They have given you their interpretation of the perfect home. Of course, your goal is to find them a home that meets their needs. Read that again. <u>Find them a home that meets their needs.</u>
You may be fortunate to find them exactly what they've asked you to look for. They fall in love with it immediately, pay full price, and the deal closes on the target date. Congratulations!

More likely though, you'll faithfully check the MLS, call them on the rare occasion that a home appears matching their wish list, set up an appointment, show them the home and it won't be exactly what their looking for. Maybe it's the neighborhood. Maybe the rooms aren't the right size. Maybe it's the decorating. Needs work, or whatever.

What I'm trying to say is, your customer really doesn't know what they're looking for. That's why they came to you.
What they do know, is that they have outgrown their apartment. They would like to have some space around them and they would appreciate some privacy. They also want to have a reasonable commute to work.

Read between the lines. Your job is to find them the very best value in their price range. It must meet there basic needs but not necessarily all of their wants. In all likelihood, a 4 bedroom, 1 & 1/2 bath colonial with a recreation room in the basement will excite them if it's in very good condition has at least 1 acre and a garage or small barn. Maybe even a Split level with an attached garage on 1/2 acre that has a family room with a fireplace located 20 miles from their employment. Rarely, if ever will you find the buyer exactly what they 'think' they're looking for, and even rarer is the chance they'll like it if you do. As a Real Estate professional, you will quickly learn that a <u>buyer doesn't really know what they want until they see it.</u>

By knowing the inventory, you'll be able to match the buyer with a choice of the 'best' homes available in their price range. (Best, meaning competitively priced best condition, good location and meeting their basic needs.) Be on your toes, for these homes don't last long.

OK. Let's back up. You've found a buyer, had them pre-approved and discussed their needs. You've shown them say, 5 homes. They have wrote an offer and after somewhat lengthy negotiations, have had it accepted. Now what?

With a little luck, and a lot of involvement, the deal will close in approximately 4 to 6 weeks. That is, assuming any inspections required either by the buyer or lender are acceptable, all repairs, if any, have been completed, the appraisal has verified the value and the survey has been completed. (If required) Title work has been completed, the deed has been prepared and signed and the lender has coordinated the closing with the escrow agent. This is the standard procedure.

Many transactions are much more complicated. So now your deal closes. It's payday! Of course, you can't live on a paycheck every 3 or 4 months. At least, not the lifestyle you got into this business anticipating. So you'll always want

Bill Drenik

to be working with 4 or 5 buyers simultaneously. That way, you'll have transactions closing on a regular basis.

You can make a lot of money selling, but you're going to do a lot of work. A lot of running, a lot of juggling, a lot of making and breaking appointments.
It's worth it in the long run. There are agents that prefer working with buyers vs. sellers.

Personally, I feel a professional agent concentrating on listings, will always have the opportunity to sell most of those listings him or her self. Therefore, They'll have control of a transaction completely, and when it closes, they'll earn a commission from both listing and selling the property. Do the math!

Let's look into other areas you'll need to master.

The Open House

One of the best ways to get started in real estate is to master the art of holding an house open. Contrary to popular belief, **Open Houses are a tremendous source of business.**
You have an opportunity to sell your own listing, you will obtain a customer base, and most importantly, open houses give you an opportunity to meet potential sellers. *Open houses generate more listings!*

Of course, as a new agent, you have no inventory. How do you hold a house open if you don't have any listings? The obvious answer is to approach a top agent. I guarantee you they will be thrilled to help you select a home from their inventory. Caution! Be selective. **Do your homework!** The home must be priced competitively, in a good location, and have curb appeal. After all, you're volunteering your time and services. You want to be sure you'll have plenty of traffic.

Schedule the open at least two weeks in advance. You'll want plenty of time to prepare and to give the owners ample time to spruce up the house.
Schedule the advertising. You'll want this published prior to the date of the open as well as on the date it's held. Give the potential customers a chance to get there.

You must take many things into consideration when determining the time of the day you'll hold the open house. Usually, open houses are held on Sunday afternoon. Keep in mind that many customers will attend church services and have dinner prior to coming. If your scheduled hours make it impossible or difficult to come, you could be losing thousands of dollars. You must give them an ample window of opportunity. A minimum of 2 -3 hours is usually sufficient.

It is always a very good idea to let the neighboring property owners know you'll be holding the Home open. Do this well in advance. Many times they will have friends or relatives that might be interested. You will want to give them a chance to choose their neighbors! Post cards are a great tool!

Post a rider on your for sale sign announcing the open house at least 3 or 4 days in advance. This will give the commuters who normally travel the road plenty of notice. They too may mention your open house to friends or Co-workers. Advertise your Open House on your web site and notify potential customers via e-mail.

Have an ample supply of hand out information at the home the day of the open house. Include disclosures, plot plan, pertinent information regarding the home, demographics if possible, current interest rates and financial information. You'll want them to be able to get pre-approved on the spot if there is an interest. Be prepared for that also.

Arrive early and plan to stay late if necessary. Never rush a customer through. Always register names and telephone numbers and e-mail addresses of all potential customers. Contact each one within 24 hours, you'll be surprised at the number of people interested in the home, or the number of people that viewed the home, weren't interested, but would like to work with you to find a home.

Let the Home sell itself. Watch for interest and buying signs. Ask questions. (Ie.) Is this the area you'd prefer? Do you have a Home to sell before you can buy? Are you working with an agent? Have you been pre-approved? How soon will you be moving? What features are you looking for in a home? Etc.

By asking questions, you will be able to match them up with another home, if the one your holding open doesn't appeal to them. Secure the customer! That's your job! You're providing a service to each person walking through the front door as well as to the owner.

Remember each potential buyer is also a potential seller. Be Professional, factual, and loaded with information. Be prepared to write an offer, discuss property values, a marketing plan, financing, pricing or to answer any other questions.

Be cordial, you'll want to do more listening than talking. Make the customer comfortable with you. Sell yourself as the knowledgeable professional they'll want to work with either now or in the near future.

Open Houses are a tremendous source of business.
Hold your listings open! You might sell it yourself, or possibly get other listings from it, which create other buyers with other homes to sell, which create other buyers with other homes to sell and on and on. You're unstoppable! **Your real estate machine begins to feed itself.**

Bill Drenik

Telephone techniques

Many a would- be sale or listing is lost simply because the agent answering the telephone was unable to 'warm up' the caller. Either the agent seems bothered by the caller and simply gives out basic information regarding a Home, or are the pre-programmed relocated 'car salesman' type Nitwit. Their mission, on each and every call, is to drill the daylights out of every caller in a robot like manner, take immediate control, accumulate facts and figures, get a name and telephone number and promise to research the data collected and get back to the caller within 24hrs. It's not unusual for this agent to be given a fictitious name and / or telephone number.

Remember we're dealing with human beings! We've got to be compassionate.

When you answer the phone, smile! Your smile will reflect in your voice. Identify yourself and ask the caller to do likewise. You'll need their telephone number, just in case. Ask them how you can help.... Listen!!!

If they're calling on a listing, ask them to bear with you while you pull it up on the computer. Do this even if it's right in front of you. While searching, begin to share information. Go slow! "That's a lovely ranch with a great view. Were you looking for a ranch?" **Listen!!!** (You will discover the style they would most prefer, and in all likelihood, the reason)

49

"How long have you been looking for a home?" **Listen!** (You'll discover their motivation and whether or not they are working with another agent)

"Is there a particular area you'd prefer?" **Listen!!!** (Very important information) "I've always liked that area myself. I've sold several homes there. Is that close to your place of employment?" (You're reaching common ground, establishing your professionalism and expressing concern for their convenience.)

"OK, I have the home on the monitor now. It's very attractive. The asking price is $149,900. Is that within your price range?" **Listen!!!** (This may give you an opportunity to explain the importance of pre-approval and an opportunity to offer to arrange this service.)

"It has a family room, 3 bedrooms, 2.5 Baths with a master and a 2 car attached garage. Is that about what you're looking for?" **Listen!!** (Now you'll learn their basic needs)

"Do you have children?" **Listen!!!** (People love to talk about their kids. Let the caller talk. You'll learn ages, sexes, accomplishments, interest etc.)

"Where do your children attend school?" **Listen!!** (Now you're closing in) "Do you live far from the school?" (Bingo! your about to get the callers address)

"I'm very familiar with that area. I've sold several homes there recently." (Reaffirming your professionalism)

"There are several homes in the _____ area that I think you may be interested in. Would you prefer an evening appointment or is Saturday morning better for you?" (You've captured the caller's interest, provided and received vital information and established yourself. They'll be happy to work with you.)

"Shall I pick you up or would you like to meet at my office? I'll need a few minutes before we get started to explain agency policies and I'd like to offer you my exclusive representation."
"It's been a pleasure talking with you. I'm looking forward to finding you the perfect home. I'll see you at my office Saturday morning."

Of course, all calls and callers are different. What you want to remember is take your time. Don't be all business. Give the caller a chance to be comfortable with you. You'll have plenty of opportunity to distinguish yourself as a knowledgeable professional. Be sure you also distinguish yourself as a caring individual.

The caller may also be interested in selling. Ideally, they'll say. "I'd like to put my Home on the market. Could you come over this afternoon? When an agent receives this call, it's usually quite a spectacle, especially if they are a member of the 90% club.

Instant panic comes to mind. They'll usually go directly into hyperventilation followed immediately by 15 minutes of breathing into a paper bag. After they've 'collected' themselves, the fun starts. After drinking between 4 and 6 glasses of water, they'll go directly to the nearest computer and start researching.
Before too long, they're standing ankle deep in nonessential data as an exhausted printer continuously spits out reams

and reams of information. Of course, there's no time to read any of it so they gather it all up, neatly pack it into their briefcase, and continue to prepare.

They've got to get a listing package together. Of course, it's been so long since the last time this happened they haven't any idea what it may contain, or how to fill the documents out. If you're within 25 feet, you get recruited to assist them. What's this document for? Do we really need this? Where do I get that information? Would you mind grabbing a sign for me? How do I get to the property address? What do you think it's worth? Etc. For the next 45 minutes or so, they'll want total silence. You'll see them agonize over documents, head in hand. A cold sweat usually follows as time draws near.

Ready or not, here I come and, out the door they go. With any luck at all, they'll manage to get the property listed.

More likely, when you get a call from a potential seller, the main concern will be. "How much do you guys charge to sell a house?"

OK, relax, this will take some time. Again, you've got to warm up the seller. He's obviously shopping around looking for a desperate agent willing to work for nothing. Rest assured, if you let him go he'll find one. You need to get an appointment. You've got to assess the situation. You need an opportunity to 'sell' yourself as a knowledgeable professional.

"Before I can answer that question, I'll need a little information."

Give the caller your name, ask him to write it down. Get the callers name and the address of the property.

"I've sold several homes in that area. How long have you lived in the home?" (Determine whether the caller actually owns the home, and potential equity)

"Tell me about the house." (Bedrooms, baths, lot size, style, age, amenities)

"Have you made any improvements recently?" (Roof, windows, siding, carpeting, etc.)

"Sounds like a great house for a ___. (Large family, first time buyer, retired couple, professional family, handyman, etc.) Would you agree with that?"

"Our commission is based upon the services we provide, the asking price and the length of time on the market. How soon will you be moving?" (Determine motivation)

"Will you be staying in the area, or relocating?" (Sellers, in many cases become Buyers)

"Has the home been on the market before?" (If so, price may be the problem. If not, price is the answer.)

"Why are you selling?" (Upsize, downsize, transferred, estate, divorce, lost a job, losing the house, opportunity to buy another, too much work, retiring south etc.)(Reinforce their motivation, and zero in on price)

To this point, you've asked the important questions. Who? What? When? Where? and Why? The important question remains. How much?

"Mr. Seller, there's only one more thing to do before I can determine the commission we'll be able to charge to sell your property. I'll stop by and have a look at the Home, evaluate the competition, and then I'll have an answer for you. Will this afternoon at 4:00 be good for you?

"But all I want to know is how much you charge."

"I understand that. The costs involved in selling a home can sometimes be quite high, but price is not cost. **You'll want to be sure you're getting your moneys worth.** We feel the same way. Our marketing expense is quite high, we'll discuss our marketing strategy and go over our fee structure when we meet. **I'll need to evaluate your needs and discuss with you <u>which services you'll want us to provide.</u>** I'll be able to give you a very accurate cost analysis and most importantly, determine your net proceeds.

<u>Our goal is the same as yours.</u> **To sell the Home at the highest price and in the shortest amount of time.** That is your goal isn't it?"

Of course it will be. You've said everything he wants to hear, but you never have answered his question.

"I'm glad you called. It's been nice talking with you. I look forward to meeting you this afternoon. I'm sure we'll be able to reach an agreement?"

When you arrive, be prompt! Above all, be prepared. Know the neighborhood. Know the asking price, selling price and days on the market of each Home sold recently as well as the amenities of each home. Know the asking price of comparable Homes on the market right now and the length of time they've been for sale.

Allow the seller to give you the grand tour. Show an interest and find a common ground. Comment on distinguishing features of the Home, he'll appreciate you noticing. Take plenty of notes and measurements.

When you sit down with the seller, be able to explain the importance of 'pricing' the Home competitively as well as the 'perils' of overpricing. Discuss your agencies marketing plan. How does your company compare with your competitors? Will you advertise locally as well as at arms length? What about MLS services, Internet sites, or exclusive advertising provided to your companies clients? Do you have a personal marketing program? What percentage of your listings sell, and what is the average marketing time? Discuss the benefit of a warranty plan and how it can increase the selling price as well as decrease the market time. Assure the seller that you have a program in place that enables you to have the buyer approved to purchase the Home before they've ever seen it. Give an example of what might happen without this benefit. Discuss your willingness to hold Open Houses.

Throughout your discussion, go slow. Encourage the seller to ask questions or make suggestions. You are forming a partnership and together, will get the job done.

Explain the standard commission for a property in this price range and the other costs involved in selling the home. If there is still an objection, ask the seller which service or services you've described previously that he wouldn't want your company to provide. In all likelihood, you'll have convinced this seller that your services are valuable and more importantly, that you are a professional. If not, keep talking. Explain the appraisal process, inspections that may be required, repairs that may be necessary, State mandated disclosures, Title guarantees, escrow services, earnest money, negotiations, title transfer and possession dates.

Bill Drenik

You're giving this guy a lot to think about. He's beginning to realize the complexities involved. Finish up with the co-broke procedure, commission splits, buyer representation and agents that only show properties offering higher commissions. Believe it or not, they're out there.

Have confidence. Be professional. In all likelihood, you'll walk away with a very saleable listing. There's a good chance you'll also be the selling agent. **Remember:** Your job is extremely complicated. Reducing a commission will not reduce the workload.

The nicest home on the street vs. the worst home on the street.

If you're going to become a top agent in real estate, you'll need to understand the importance and the difference in location and price. A very large percentage of real estate agents seem to confuse the two.

Consider for example, a street in the suburbs of any town, in any state consisting of single family homes built between 1980 and 1990. On this particular street, there are two Homes currently for sale.

These two Homes are located directly across from each other, were both built in 1985 and are on identical sized lots. Each owner bought their home brand new and paid approximately $100,000. The homes are similar in style and square footage. Mr. & Mrs. Smith live on the East side of the street and Mr. & Mrs. Jones on the West. The average value of a Home on this street is now $175,000.

Mr. & Mrs. Smith have always shown tremendous pride in ownership. There Home is professionally landscaped and meticulously kept. They have recently replaced the roof and central air conditioning unit and had new siding and windows installed. The interior of their home is impeccable, professionally decorated and recently carpeted wall to wall. Within the past two years, they have installed a new kitchen and updated both bathrooms. The Home is definitely a showplace, the nicest on the street. In 1998, their Home received an 'Owners Pride' plaque which is proudly hanging on the front door. They are retiring and downsizing. They have decided that since their home is unquestionably the best on the street. They would put it on the market for $225,900.

Mr. & Mrs. Jones' house hasn't faired as well. It is in need of a roof replacement and the paint is beginning to peel. The windows are original and inefficient. The shrubbery they planted 10 years ago is overgrown and the cracked driveway is in need of resurfacing. The garage door is broken and remains half open at all times. The interior of the Home has the original carpeting. It is badly worn, as are the hardwood floors in the dining room. Windowsills are scratched, the screens on the front door are torn. There is a definite pet odor. They have 2 dogs, several cats and 4 children. The walls are dirty and damaged. The kitchen is sufficient but the cabinetry is tired. The dishwasher hasn't worked for 3 years. There is a stain on the living room ceiling caused by a leak in the upstairs bathroom. The leak has been repaired but the stain remains. They have recently replaced the furnace and hot water tank. They do not have central air. Mr. Jones has been transferred out of state. They need a quick sale. They realize the home needs work. They have Contractors estimates of $35,000 and $42,000 to refurbish the home. They do not have the money nor the time to have the work done. Their agent, Tommy Toplister has assessed the situation.

If the Jones' make the necessary repairs and improvements, their
home would be worth approximately $175,000. Allowing $40,000 for the work to be performed and $3500 for

central air would place the value of the Jones' home at approximately $131,500 as is. However, since the Smiths Home is listed at $229,000, and it's directly across the street he suggests a list price of $150,000. He realizes the Home is slightly overpriced but in comparison to the Smith home, it still seems to be a very good value. The Home is livable, but needs immediate cosmetic attention. In all likelihood, a discreet potential buyer will view both Homes before making an offer.

Both Homes are overpriced, but the Smith Home at $229,000 has a positive or pulling effect on the value of the Jones'. (It would have this effect whether overpriced or not) The Jones Home has the very same pulling effect on the Smith Home. But the results are negative, pulling the value downward.

In all likelihood, The Jones Home will sell relatively fast. They will be thrilled to accept an offer between $140,000 and $145,000. The buyer of their home will see the potential of increasing the value of the Home by painting, carpeting and landscaping. Of course the roof would have to be replaced right away but other repairs could be made over the course of time. Possibly by the buyers themselves. What about the Smith Home?

It will probably linger on the market for quite some time. They'll more than likely change real estate companies after 6 months and reduce the price to $219,000. Six months later, when Mr. Smith decides to sell it by-owner He'll reduce the price again to $209,000. By this time, The Buyers of the Jones' Home have completed the refurbishing of their new Home.

The roof, siding, windows, carpeting, central air and landscaping were all contracted out at a price of $26,000. They completed the interior work themselves at a cost of $3,900. Their Home was recently appraised for $180,000 which is now the average price of Homes on the street.

Tommy Toplister has been talking with the Smiths and they have agreed to allow him a one-time showing. His customer makes an offer of $195,000.00 which the Smiths reluctantly accept. However, Tommy had to agree to a reduced commission of 5%. A disappointed Mr. Smith grumbles. "I could have got <u>that much</u> for the property 1.5 years ago." Tommy smiles....

Considering the mortgage payment, taxes, utilities and insurance the Smiths paid over the past 1.5 years, they would have been much farther ahead had they priced the home more competitively and sold it much sooner.

The location of a property will always reflect in its value.
<u>Location, Location, Location.</u>
However, the attraction of the location has more affect on the price a buyer will be willing to pay for a property than the price a seller will get for their property.

Price, Price, Price

Suppose your local bakery sells loaves of bread for $1.00 each. The bread always sells quickly because it's baked fresh every day. The loaves are always identical because they are mass produced.

One day, the baker decides he will make some bread by hand. He puts his heart and soul into making the bread. He mixed the ingredients precisely, kneaded the dough to perfection and baked it with pride. When finished, he decides that this is the very best bread he's ever made. It may look like every other loaf, but this bread is special.

He decides to charge $2.00 for the hand made loaves. The loaves are placed in the showcase side by side.

"Some are $1.00 and some are $2.00. They look exactly the same." Exclaimed a regular customer."What's so special about the $2.00 loaves?" She asks. "I made them from scratch, completely by hand." Says the baker. "Bread is bread." Says the customer and takes a $1.00 loaf. And so it went.

Two days later, the baker has still has all of the $2.00 loaves. He decides to reduce the price to $1.50.

The same customer comes along. "I'm curious what's so special about your hand made loaves?" She says. "I'll give you $1.25"

"Never!" Says the baker. "I made these loaves myself, completely from scratch. You've never tasted bread this good". He says. "Bread is bread" says the customer as she buys another $1.00 loaf.

Two days later she's back again. The price of the hand made bread is now $1.00 per loaf, the same as the mass-produced bread. The hand made bread has gotten hard and stale. The mass produced bread is soft and fresh. How much would <u>you</u> pay for the hand made bread?

When a Home is overpriced, it has the same effect. It will get a lot of attention at first, then hardly any until the price begins to fall. When it does get to the price it should have been listed at originally, there is no longer any interest in it. It has become stale. Even if it now becomes a value, there is a stigma attached to it. "There must be something wrong with the house or it would have sold long ago etc." The reluctant owner will either 'give it to another real estate company, usually at the same inflated listing price, take it off the market, or accept an inferior offer.

To sell a Home quickly and realize the highest possible selling price, a Home must be priced competitively.

Competitively priced Homes generate interest. Interest generates offers. ***The closer a Home is priced to the market value, the higher the offer will be.*** Many times, the Home that is 'priced to sell', will generate multiple offers for the owner, sometimes driving the selling price above the asking price.

Overpriced Homes on the other hand will help sell everyone else's listing but yours. ***Price, Price, Price,*** The three most important words in real estate.

Bill Drenik

Pricing

Keep the previous analogy in mind, and use it. If you know you're facing a difficult presentation, don't hesitate to bring 2 loaves of bread with you. You'll definitely break the ice, make your point, and have something to eat if it turns into a marathon.

Another important consideration when pricing a Home is it's exterior appearance or 'curb appeal'. Unless the backyard is facing a breathtaking view such as mountains, a valley or lakefront, the price *must reflect the appearance of the Home.*

If the Home is drop dead gorgeous on the inside, but plain Jane on the outside, you're going to have a problem.

You must have the patience and tenacity to spend whatever time is necessary to educate the seller on the importance of pricing. The listing price must be competitive with similar Homes in the area. **I promise you that all the advertising in the world will not convince a would-be customer to want to view a Home that doesn't look as if it's worth the asking price.** The price must reflect the exterior appearance or the Home will see no activity.

Keep remembering and remind yourself constantly. **You're a Top Agent.** You're focus and purpose as a top agent is to acquire listings that will sell. Pricing is the key.

Bill Drenik

Who sets the price

The value of a Home is not determined by the Real Estate Agent nor is it determined by the owner.

The market sets the price. You must do a thorough study of the current market to prepare to counsel the owner. Together, you will analyze the data, establish the *'target selling price'*, and discuss a marketing plan. Only then, will you, and the seller, be confident in the fact that the property is priced fairly and competitively.

Many factors must be considered. Style, size, age, setting, location, condition and amenities such as bedrooms, baths, fireplace, garage, family room, basement, crawl space etc.

Also consider recently sold properties, the number of days on the market, expired listings and the reasons they did not sell.

Other influences on value include interest rates, financing available, time of the year and the abundance of homes on the market.

Pricing is critical!! An overpriced home will accelerate the sale of a reasonably priced comparable home. An overpriced home will most likely be reduced several times before selling or stagnate and expire. If and when it does sell, it will be for much less than it's actually worth.

Try to compare the Home with a similar, *recently sold* home. Never compare the Home with another home on the market that is overpriced. **Your listing needs to be the best value in its price range and area.**

Personal Marketing

In your area, wherever that may be, you will readily recognize the names of a handful of real estate agents.
You probably think that these are supermen and women that have undoubtedly been in the business for years.

You see their names and faces on shopping carts, in newspapers and magazines. You hear their ads on the radio and sometimes see them on cable TV. Their personal ads are on menus, bulletins, sports programs and billboards. You'll see their names on everything, tee shirts, ink pens, key chains, balloons and license plates. You instantly associate their names with real estate and success.

Whenever I've mentioned the 10% of real estate agents that do 90% of the business, their faces and names drift through your mind. They are who you're trying to be.

Listen up! - Get closer, **this is important.**
Without a doubt, these are members of the 10% club. However, they have not necessarily been in the business very long at all.

They have created a *perception of professionalism* with a comprehensive personal marketing strategy.

This type of strategy is guaranteed to catapult you to the top of your profession, **if sustained**. Very few agents will reach the top pinnacles of the profession without a personal marketing plan.

You can do this at any stage of your career, the question is, Why wait? Determine your market, market your face and set up an annual budget and marketing plan.

Your brokerage will do a fabulous job of advertising the listings you acquire, but you will be sorely disappointed if you think they're going to excessively advertise your face and name. You must do that yourself!

Advertising is costly to be sure. However, if your advertising effectively combines your listings with your name and face, you will create a continuous perception of being a premier agent, one of the best in the business.

You can't do it all. You've got to start on a small but realistic scale. A business card sized ad running continuously in your local newspaper will begin to establish your recognition. You'll be surprised how many people you know will recognize you. Your personal marketing will help them to remember to refer you if they have an opportunity.

The key is to be constant. If you advertise yourself sporadically, you will be wasting your money. Remember, for the most part, your training will come from experience. The more business you produce, the more experience you'll receive and the more professional you'll become.

Once you've established yourself, every $1.00 you spend on you personal marketing campaign, if, and only if it's constant, will pay big dividends in commissions earned.

Create a perception. The perception becomes real.

Think long term

As a real estate professional, you will be working, *'whenever you're not sleeping'.*

Wherever you go, whatever you do, always consider yourself available.
You may be filling your gas tank, eating lunch at a Diner or cutting your grass. Wherever you are, whenever you have the opportunity to meet or talk to people, you are working.

Always be prepared. You will be surprised at the number of people who will consider you their authority in matters considering real estate.

Never expect instant gratification from your advice or service. You've got to think long term. Your product is your service. You must constantly sell your product. *Be aware,* you are under a microscope. Everything you do, everything you say, the company you keep, the places you go, the clothes you wear etc. all make an impression. A combination of making the right impression and creating the right perception will supply business both today, and tomorrow.

Be your best. Do your best, and try your best. Always give 100%. Like any product, if it's well received, people will recommend you to others. Just as a satisfied customer can help your future business, a dissatisfied customer can hurt it. *Think long term.*

Bill Drenik

Knock on doors

It never ceases to amaze me at the amount of business that can be generated by spending a few hours on a sunny afternoon, walking door to door, introducing yourself.

What amazes me even more, is the high percentage of agents (probably 90%) that won't do it.

I will say again, what I've tried to say many times before. **You are working for yourself.** You must do whatever works to generate business. The more agents that refuse to do the techniques that work, the better it is for you, if you're compelled to become a top agent.

By now I hope you realize that you must lead and not follow to succeed, the formula is simple. *Do what works!*

Let's take a street in your neighborhood and knock on a few doors. Chose any street, it always works. For this particular street let's assume there are 20 homes on each side of the street.
Plan to spend 1.5 - 2 hours going door to door introducing yourself. You're simply going to introduce yourself, exchange pleasantries, hand them your business card and ask if they're thinking of selling in the near future. ***That's it.*** Don't complicate it.

A high percentage will simply say ''no''. That's fine, and to be expected. Thank them for their time, mention that there is an increased demand for properties in the area and ask them to call you if they happen to think of anyone that might consider selling **_That's it._** Go to the next house.

You're entire presentation and conversation lasted less than 2 minutes. You might feel, at this point, that this cannot possibly work. Keep going. Let's see what happens.

You were very apprehensive at the first house. A little nervous, and it showed. As you continue down the street, things begin to change. You realize you're providing a service. You're confidence begins to build, and at each succeeding house you're refining you're presentation.

As you proceed down one side of the street and up the other, you'll meet many people. For the most part, they will be very cordial and friendly, and many will offer you leads. " We're not really thinking about selling right now but the Browns' have mentioned that they might sell this year." *Or,* "No, but if you find anyone who might sell, our daughter would love to buy in this neighborhood." *Or,* So and so are getting a divorce, outgrowing their house, thinking about retiring to Florida, etc. etc.

You will have a very productive afternoon. Again, you must think long term. As you proceed throughout the neighborhood, you are planting seeds. Think of yourself as the Johnny Appleseed of real estate. Believe me, I've gone door to door many times and there will always be someone who says, "What a coincidence, we were just discussing the possibility of selling last night." *Or,* " I'm so glad you came, we're thinking of selling and didn't know who to call."

I'm very serious, <u>it happens.</u> Real estate is a percentage game. Out of 40 homes, you're almost certain to get at least 1 owner who says yes.

OK, you've made your rounds and acquired 1 listing. That one listing will pay you quite handsomely for 2 hours of work.

What else will happen? To be sure, you will be the topic of conversation at many dinner tables tonight. "A real estate man stopped at the house this afternoon. He was asking if we wanted to sell our Home. He said that the demand is high in the area and that it's a good time to sell." *You've planted the seed.*
"Well we've lived here for twenty years, why would we want to sell now?" asks the husband. "I told him we weren't interested in selling, but you know, we've always talked about moving closer to the kids, this might not be a bad time to consider it." says the wife.
"Well how much can we get for our house?" asks the husband. "He didn't say. He was very nice though. I see that He's listed the Browns house down the street. I can call him and ask the price" she says. "Well, why don't you do that tomorrow. I'm still not sure we should consider selling though." he says. "I know, I'm not either, Just curious I guess" she says.

The next evening... - " I called the real estate agent today, he's very nice, the Browns Home is listed at $145,900. It was shown 3 times today and he thinks an offer might be coming in." She says.

"That's incredible" says the husband, ''I had no idea the values went up so much. This just *might* be the time to sell. Why don't you call the agent tomorrow. It wouldn't hurt to know what our Home is worth, would it?"

This scenario will repeat itself over and over again. You'll be receiving calls from people on that particular street for weeks, months, and even years. Some will decide to sell. Others will give you names of potential buyers, or leads in other neighborhoods or areas. They will call with questions concerning real estate, they will recommend you and remember you.

Keep your name in front of them. Notes, postcards or a return visit will ensure you are remembered. ***You have become the expert in the neighborhood.***

Knocking on doors <u>will</u> produce business. It will also establish your confidence and professionalism. It's also a great way to get into the habit of telling everyone you meet that you are an agent, an opportunity to give them your card and ask them for business.

Business is everywhere. You've got to find it! You must get out and look for it. Be continuously alert and search for opportunity. Become a real estate detective.

'Sherlock' Realtor

You'll be surprised at how many potential listings you can discover by simple observation. Train yourself to look for telltale signs.

If you suspect a home is vacant, you need to investigate. Homes left unattended can mean many things. The property may be in foreclosure, and abandoned. The owners may have separated or divorced. The owner may no longer be able to maintain or care for the home. The owner may live out of town, or out of state. The tenants may have moved out. The Home may be an estate. The owner may have been transferred.

All of the reasons above, and many more, result in homes being left vacant and unattended. When you see a home that appears vacant, check it out!

The neighbors will usually know the history of the home. Don't hesitate to ask, trust me, they will gladly share the information with you. In fact, they'll probably tell you much more than you'll need to know.

What you want to learn, is the address of the owner or caretaker if it's different from the home address. If you're unable to ascertain this information from the neighbors, get a legal description of the property with a <u>tax mailing address.</u> If the tax mailing address is the same as the property address, send a registered letter to the owner. It will be forwarded to them. If the tax mailing address is different from the property address, get a telephone number from the information operator and call them. If the number is unlisted, send a registered letter.

You can suspect a property is empty if the grass is overgrown and there's trash in the yard. Curtains may be missing or hanging strangely. A window may be broken or a door ajar. The home may need obvious repairs or may be in an unfinished state of repair. In the winter, the driveway may be unplowed, you probably won't see smoke coming from the chimney or you may see frost on the interior of the windows, etc.

An empty home is a potential listing. It is in the owners' best interest to sell the home rather than leave it unattended. There are ongoing cost involved, incurred whether a home is vacant or occupied.

When you do discover the owner, call and discuss the situation with them. Tell them why you suspect the home is vacant and ask if you could help. There is a very high risk involved to the owner of a vacant home. They will be concerned about security, vandalism and theft. They have utility costs, insurance costs, a possible mortgage payment and tax liability. You're doing them a great favor by calling. They may not even know the home is vacant. Once you've discovered the owners' name, address, or telephone number. Make immediate contact and keep in touch. Your detective work may result in another listing.

Another place 'Sherlock' Realtor may discover listings is through a lender. Banks, Mortgage Companies, Finance companies and Private lenders all have a constant inventory of

Real Estate Owned properties. (REO's) These are properties which the Lender has acquired through foreclosure, deed in lieu or bankruptcy. These properties are a burden to the lenders because of the ongoing costs and risks mentioned previously. Every lender will have their share of these properties.

Let's face it. People sometimes stretch their budget pretty tight in order to buy a home. In recent years, with interest rates being so low, with lenders willing to finance as much as 125% of the value of the purchase, and with the constant invitation to refinance, sometimes people get in over their heads. There may be a cutback in overtime, layoff, termination, or strike that affects the income of the owner. An accident, medical emergency, or other financial tragedy may initiate a series of late or missed payments that eventually results in foreclosure. Divorces and separations can lead to financial ruin, neglected payments, bankruptcy and loss of property.

These are unfortunate circumstances to be sure. But they are frequent occurrences in this day and age.

Contact the lenders main or corporate office, the local branch may not have knowledge of the REO inventory. Ask for the *Real Estate Owned* department. Discuss the inventory in your area with the REO representative. They will willingly give you information, and welcome your help in selling these homes. You must call continuously, at least once per month. The inventory is constant. Eventually, you can expect to begin to acquire listings in your area from the lender. Once you've established yourself with the firm, doors will begin to open even further. **Investigate the possibilities!**

Another source of listing leads is of course, Attorneys.

Attorneys oversee bankruptcies, estates and divorces. You on the other hand will at times be asked to recommend a real estate attorney to protect your customers or clients' interest in a property exchange. A referral relationship with an established firm can be profitable. The same is true of CPA's. At times, their clients' portfolio may be unbalanced in such a way that selling a property, or buying additional investment properties would make financial sense. You will of course want these clients referred to you. Don't overlook nursing homes or assisted living centers. They will usually have an inventory of real estate they have taken as payment in the event a senior citizen, without heirs, and without assets other than real estate, is in need of immediate long term care.

Stay Alert! - The possibilities are everywhere.

On the road again

If you're fortunate enough to be the only real estate agent to be living in a popular allotment containing say, 500 Homes, there is an excellent chance that you will be able to establish yourself as 'the' allotment real estate professional. You will be handling all the listings and sales within the allotment. You'll enjoy an exceptionally lucrative career. That is, until you sell a home to another agent, or to someone who decides to become an agent, or until other agents decide to invade your territory.

In short, *it's not gonna happen.* If you are going to succeed, resolve yourself to the fact that you will have to be mobile. Business will not come to you. You have to go out and get it.

A tremendous number of agents will establish invisible boundaries for themselves. They may have decided to be an agent in a town with a population of 10,000 people who live in 3,500 homes of which 225 will sell each year. Of course, There will be 50 other agents in that town and 5 of them will do 90% of the business.

Do the math. The 5 top agents in town will sell a combined total of 202 Homes. That leaves 23 homes for the other 45 agents to sell. Most will of course realize they have to expand their parameters to neighboring towns in order to maintain their existence. Others, believe it or not, will continue to 'wait' for the banner year in which 10 of their relatives or friends all decide to make a move.

Take a minute now and look behind you. You see, there's no anchor back there, and you're not chained to your desk. You're free to go, wherever you need to go to find business.

I have observed and you will too, agents who hand other agents tens of thousand of commission dollars each and every year because the Home they were asked to list, or to show was too far away. I'm not talking about hundreds of miles. I've known agents who won't travel 20 miles. Needless to say, this is bad practice.

When opportunity presents itself to you. Gas up and go! You cannot travel even 5 miles, in any direction without passing countless other opportunities. You'll pass Fsbo's for sure. You'll probably pass vacant homes. The owners of the home you're going out to may become a buyer and the buyer of the home you're going out to list or show may also become a seller.
(Another listing opportunity)

You may be unfamiliar with the area you're asked to service, therefore, uncomfortable with values.
That's not an acceptable excuse. You have the MLS at your service. A competitive market analysis of the similar homes in a given area will always narrow the range of value. You can work anywhere!
Never limit yourself by territory. $5.00 worth of gas can turn into thousands of dollars of income, unlock other opportunities and grow your business.

A busy agent is a happy agent. Always be available.

Part time agent

OK, you've got a decent job, but you don't make enough money. Or, you're a few years from retirement and you're looking for a second career. Maybe you're a housewife whose children are in high school and you need a second income or feel compelled to get back into the workforce. For whatever the reason, real estate looks good to you. If you get licensed, what can you expect?

Certain individuals can supplement their income quite handsomely when they become a real estate agent, <u>if,</u> they take advantage of the opportunities presented to them on a daily basis.

For the most part, there is no such thing as a part time real estate agent. As I've stated before, an agent is working, whenever they're not sleeping. The trick is <u>*not to sleep with your eyes wide open!*</u>

You might work in a factory, or in an office. Maybe you're a teacher, truck driver, construction worker, nurse, engineer, waitress, cab driver, butcher, baker or candlestick maker.

Maybe you don't work at all, but you're a member of the PTA, a scout leader, a Hospital volunteer or a member of a church. It doesn't matter. What does matter is that you are in contact with people. These people are your sphere of influence. You must farm them constantly. <u>Your conversations must always contain real estate.</u>

Don't forget your co-workers. **You must work very hard to convince them that you are a misplaced full time real estate agent working with them on a part time basis.**

You've got to tell them continuously that you're an agent, and continuously ask for their business and referrals.

Of course, **you must specialize in *listing*** properties. You'll have no time to show homes, Your part time obligation to their fraternity forbids it. However, you have an army of agents at your side, each with an entourage of buyers wanting to purchase a Home just like theirs. Etc.

If a 'part time' agent is likable, alert, outgoing, knowledgeable, assertive, hard working, honest, patient, convincing, dedicated, determined and has made a decision to survive, they should be able to supplement their income quite nicely.

If, however, you're intent is to get a real estate license and sell real estate to, and for, your relatives and friends. *Forget it right now*. You'll not only starve, but you'll probably be disowned, and possibly tarred and feathered.

Remember, when you are a licensed agent, you become an independent contractor. *You're in business for yourself.* There are going to be cost involved. The same basic costs apply whether you are a Top Agent, bottom agent or part time agent.

Let's look closer at what some of these costs might be and how spending a dime today can make you a lot of dollars tomorrow.

<u>*The cost to stay in business*</u>

A real estate agent is, an independent business person.

You will represent a brokerage, but *your income will come exclusively as a result of your own efforts.* Like all businesses, there are costs involved.

Getting your license is relatively inexpensive considering the fact that *once licensed, you have unlimited earning potential.*

Additional fees that you will have, include but are not limited to, the following. Check with your manager for specific costs.

1. Join the board of Realtors. Usually a first time initiation fee, then an ongoing annual fee.
2. You must be a member of the Multiple Listing Service to access. - Usually a monthly fee. You can join more than one if necessary in your area.
3. Annual license renewal fee.
4.Your brokerage may require a technical usage fee, or require a monthly advertising contribution.

These are basic costs and relatively inexpensive. Remember however, these costs start immediately, not when you start closing transactions.

To realize your dream, to become a **Top Agent,** you'll need to invest considerably more into your business. Technological advances have elevated the profession to new heights enabling Top agents to enhance their performance, increase their production and separate themselves from the field.

Caution. Don't spend money needlessly. Tools, and toys are worthless until you're comfortable and know how to use them.
Introduce technology into your business that will help your performance <u>now</u>.

It is wise to invest a portion of each commission check you receive back into your business. Start slow, but grow steady. ***<u>Concentrate on personal promotion.</u>*** The more business you can create for yourself, the more tools you can implement into your business.
You're in business. You ***must*** think of it that way.

<u>Other expenses you'll need to grow into</u>:

1. Cell phone - Call the Fsbo's from their driveway.
2. Personal computer - The MLS at your Home office.
3. Notebook computer - Take your office with you.
4. Digital camera
5. Software programs - Top producer, Top presenter
6. Sign riders - Promote yourself.
7. Information boxes, Talking House, Internet web page, etc.
8. Newsletters, personal postcards, Motivational seminars.
9. Personal assistant or Partnership.
10. Internet access is a must. <u>Put this first on your list.</u>

There are always tools to enhance and promote your business.

The faster you grow. *The farther you'll go!*

Bill Drenik

It's lonely at the top

By now, I hope you realize that you ***can*** be a top agent. You are not entering a profession in which you climb the ladder to success based on tenor or seniority. You can actually enter the world of real estate at the top and remain there if you exhibit the tenacity.

There is nothing, and no one that can keep you from accomplishing your goal. There are however, three prerequisites.

1. You must make a *decision* to be a Top Agent.
2. You must be *determined* to be a Top Agent.
3. You must be *dedicated* to your profession, clients & customers.

The 3 **D's**, - *Decision, Determination* and *Dedication.*

You cannot, and will not, become a top real estate agent unless ***and until***, you possess all three.

Almost anyone can become a real estate agent. You take the required courses, pass an exam, and voila', you're an agent!

That's not your goal or purpose. You want to have a rewarding, exciting, challenging but, lucrative career.

Deciding to be a Real Estate Agent, is relatively simple. Deciding to be a **Top** Real Estate Agent is a different matter altogether.

Bill Drenik

Once you've made the **decision** that you're going to succeed, that you will do whatever you have to, *whatever it takes* to become successful in real estate, you're already halfway there. From that point on, you must be **determined** to succeed.

You will experience many set backs along the way. Each will contain a valuable lesson. Let's face it. *Mistake is the greatest teacher*. **You must not give up!**

You must be **dedicated** to service, *available when called upon.*

You'll need to possess the ability to humble yourself if necessary to achieve the goals set by others. You must be willing to be thorough, accurate, punctual, sacrificing and serious. You must develop a passion for helping others.

Focus on your goal. Others will try to discourage you. Push through it! You can do it.

Warning: Every agent before you, and the majority of those to come, will have entered the world of real estate with a determination to succeed and a promise of dedicated service.

Only the **top agents** made a conscious *decision* to be successful.

And they are!

<u>*Expect the worst*</u>

I couldn't possibly pass on the opportunity to express a life-learned philosophy that will consistently deliver a source of redemption.

Have a positive attitude, but **expect the worst!**

I don't mean this to sound cynical, I do mean however, that you must proceed with extreme caution on behalf of your customers and clients.

Selling, or purchasing a home is a highly emotional experience. You will be trusted to facilitate the transition properly, to protect your clients' integrity, to conduct yourself professionally, to carry the burden of stress and to preserve a reasonable continuance of their lifestyle throughout the transaction.

The agent involved has a responsibility to foresee potential problems that may arise in the sale or purchase, forewarn the client of the possibilities, discuss solutions and ramifications, and resolve, if possible, any perplexities that may arise.

When you expect the worst, your client or customer can expect, *and will get*, the best.

A lot of things can happen between acceptance of an offer and title transfer.

*   The Buyers loan may be denied.

* A house sale contingency may fall through.
* Buyers remorse
* Sellers remorse
* Breach of contract
* The septic system may fail inspection.
* Undisclosed assessments may be discovered.
* Mineral right leases might turn up.
* The water might be contaminated.
* Incorrect MLS information. (Ie.) Square footage, lot size.
* Low appraisal
* There may be an easement or encroachment.
* The county engineer may require a new survey.
* Zoning may prohibit intended usage.
* Termite damage, powder post beetles, bee infestation etc.
* A home inspection may disclose unacceptable conditions that require repairs.
* Roof leaks.
* Inadequate or unsafe electrical service.
* Furnace unsafe.
* Stair handrails.
* Peeling paint.
* Unsafe walkways.
* Inoperable windows
* Radon gas
* Lead base paint
* Mechanics liens
* Sibling rivalry/ Spousal separation
* Partnership disagreements.
* Loss of employment

You get the picture. Usually, repairs, concessions or re-negotiations can overcome obstacles such as these. Prepare your client in advance, of worst case scenarios such as those listed. When you do, and problems arise, it won't be the end of the world, nor the end of your relationship. In fact, your professional representation will be elevated to new heights. You will be highly regarded and regularly referred.

On the other hand, suppose you don't inform them of possible issues that may effect the sale. They box up their belongings, put a down payment on another house, maybe reserve a moving company etc. In their hearts and minds, their house is sold and their dreams have relocated.

When problems arise, ***all hell will break loose***. Tensions, stress and frustrations will mount. Anger will surface and ***you*** will take the blame. Their dreams will be shattered, at least temporarily. The problem may be resolved, but you will bear the scars. You're completely innocent of course, after all, you don't own the House and you're not trying to buy it. However, you did fail to caution them and therein lies the rub.

This experience will be recalled as a nightmare. You will be associated with it. Do you think you'll get referrals?

Remember, you cannot make decisions for the Seller or Buyer. Their signed agreement is legal, binding and enforceable. Problems will arise. There is almost always a solution. Selling or buying real estate is emotional.

Your customer and client can ***Expect the best,*** but only if you expect and are prepared for, the worst.

<u>Go for it</u>

If you're still reading this handbook, you've probably got a chance. Before you take the next step though, think it through.
I'm not kidding, this is a tough business, but it's not rocket science. You can do it!

You're reading this handbook for the same reason I'm writing it. ***<u>We both want you to be successful.</u>***

If you're a self-starter, adventurous, curious or compelled, if you know people, like people or like to meet people, **this is for you!**

There is an increasing need for Real Estate professionals. With over 6 billion people on this planet, there will always be a demand for housing. Job security is guaranteed. Opportunities are everywhere!

This handbook is meant to give you an insight into the world of real estate, to help you decide if you have what it takes to be successful. If so**, you <u>can</u> realize your dreams**.

Do you want to own your own business? Are you ready to accept the responsibilities?
Can you sell yourself? Will underachievers distract you? Will rejection motivate you, or destroy you?

If you're serious about a career in real estate, I'm confident this handbook will give you a definite advantage. Consider it to be a blueprint for building a successful career, or at the very least, a solid foundation.

Congratulations on your decision to become a <u>*successful*</u> real estate professional! Welcome to a very special group.

Your career will be rewarding, exciting, fulfilling and adventurous. Your determination to succeed and dedication to your career will soon begin to pay tremendous dividends.

You will be compensated generously and recognized as a leader amongst your peers. Whatever your dreams may be, they are now within your reach.

Set goals for yourself! As you achieve them, raise the bar. There are no limits to how far you may go, how much you can earn or how much you will learn. *You control your destiny.*

Work hard and steady. Focus on the task at hand. Be thorough in your duty. Give factual information, educated counsel, and exemplary service and you will be admired, respected, requested and referred.

You've made a wise decision. Stand tall. You are <u>*ready*</u> to enter the world of real estate.

About the Author

Bill has been practicing real estate professionally for over 20 years and loves every minute of it. He has hundreds of published real estate newsletters to his credit. He tells it like it is and shares his observations, experiences, success and failures.